Praise for *In the Bone-Cracking Cold*

"M. Bartley Seigel was and will always be a poet laureate of the Upper Peninsula. In his latest poetry collection, he writes of bodies against the backdrop of dark, cold waters and a brutal but impossibly beautiful landscape. Each word rises from the page etched, carefully, in stone. Seigel has crafted an engrossing and deeply immersive book—part love song, part monument, part elegy, wholly unforgettable."

—Roxane Gay, bestselling author of *Bad Feminist* and *Hunger*

"We might call Seigel's poems 'sacred holdings— / little haloed echoes, etched in gemstone and antler.' But that would miss the gut ache cached in these 'feral voices,' the 'dark thing' that 'hides behind the heavenly.' This haunting collection—part elegy, part praise song—is all search. The author reminds us we must first hunger before we can relish each unlikely feast."

—Kimberly Blaeser, author of *Ancient Light* and former Wisconsin Poet Laureate

"Parts of our country have often seemed to exist beyond the reaches of art and literature, and the great forest of northern Michigan is one of those places. In M. Bartley Seigel's remarkable collection, the poet braids up language and landscape, giving voice to the spirit of a place—with its frozen swamps, wildlife, militias, poverty, its culture, its delicacy, and its beauty. With formal dexterity and memorable musicality, Seigel has made an important contribution to our understanding of what it feels like to fully reside in a location beautifully contended with by the poetic imagination."

—Mark Wunderlich

"This collection pulls you into saturated, secluded intimacy with the paradoxically iconic and unknown Upper Peninsula of Michigan. M. Bartley Seigel is hospitably at home in this, offering existential, domestic, and sociopolitical meditations with the UP and Lake Superior as his scenic background and as his total reason for being; as the air and water they breathe and swim in, metaphorically and literally as Seigel does on every other page, floating 'out beyond the tree line's reflection to a place we know cannot be depended upon. Here we release our buoys from their chains so we might display our illuminated objects.' Ripples of interiority meeting real exterior space: that is what we need in a poetry of self and place. You'll find that here—one keen voice, sounding this deep corner of the Great Lakes."

—Moheb Solim--

"Near the end of this new collection, Seigel writes: 'all soft / procedure and steel // will.' It is just one moment of many where these deeply resonant poems become an eloquent landscape similar to the one in which they were made. To read *In the Bone-Cracking Cold* is to dwell in a kind of place few will know as intimately as Seigel does. Thank goodness he has made these, by turns, tender and flinty poems."

—Alison Swan, author of *A Fine Canopy* (Wayne State University Press) and *Fresh Water*

"In the bone-cracking cold we shiver and search our minds for memories and images to warm our souls. M. Bartley Seigel's new book calls to mind those moments when we see things with icy clarity. Of the many glistening lines to nourish readers in his new collection, one of my favorites is: 'In rolling waves of laughter, we rise to greet whatever sky awaits.' Seigel is a poet not afraid to greet the sky, the seasons, the stars, and all the brilliant new poems that he brings to life. Reading his work is an introduction to the northland he loves and the honesty he demands of himself. May his blessed poems continue to drift up for years to come. Ezhi-ozhibii'ang giwii-giiwemin. He has a way of leading us home."

—Margaret Noodin, author of *What the Chickadee Knows* and *Weweni* (both Wayne State University Press)

IN THE BONE-CRACKING COLD

Made in Michigan Writers Series

A complete listing of the books in this series can be found online at wsupress.wayne.edu.

IN THE BONE-CRACKING COLD

Poems by M. Bartley Seigel

WAYNE STATE UNIVERSITY PRESS
DETROIT

© 2025 by M. Bartley Seigel. All rights reserved. No part of this book may be reproduced without formal permission.

ISBN 9780814352168 (paperback)
ISBN 9780814352175 (ebook)

Library of Congress Control Number: 2024945275

Cover art © Adobe Stock. Cover design by Laura Klynstra.

Publication of this book was made possible by a generous gift from The Meijer Foundation.

Wayne State University Press rests on Waawiyaataanong, also referred to as Detroit, the ancestral and contemporary homeland of the Three Fires Confederacy. These sovereign lands were granted by the Ojibwe, Odawa, Potawatomi, and Wyandot Nations, in 1807, through the Treaty of Detroit. Wayne State University Press affirms Indigenous sovereignty and honors all tribes with a connection to Detroit. With our Native neighbors, the press works to advance educational equity and promote a better future for the earth and all people.

Wayne State University Press
Leonard N. Simons Building
4809 Woodward Avenue
Detroit, Michigan 48201-1309

Visit us online at wsupress.wayne.edu.

Contents

A Good Omen	1
I'm Told It's Foolish to Befriend a Water Lynx	2
Before the Fall	3
Ours Are These Old Stamp Mills	4
Bottled Letters to Former Lovers	5
Wave After Wave	6
Into the Thicket	7
Beach Glass	8
Wrap the Next Hour in Rice Paper	9
Little Spirits	10
Body as Burning Bush, All the Snakes	11
Nearing the End of the Anthropocene	12
Land Acknowledgment, 1842 Ceded Territory	13
Make the Shape of Michigan with Your Hands	14
At the Mouth of the Gratiot	15
Up in Uncanny Valley	16
Out Back of the Camp	17
This Survival Knife Is All We'll Need	18
Outside the U.P. Pub, Calumet, Michigan	19
Following the Fools' Coup D'état	20
Etched in Gemstone and Antler	21
We Shed Our Clothes like Leaves	22
The Drowned Forest Swallows Him	23

They Say Not to Speak of the Negatives	24
Just About Everything Begins with a Lump	25
Fourteener for the Restless in the Long Night	26
There Are Places to Hunt	27
Out Here, We're All of Us Cracked	28
Mistakes Were Made	29
Ars Poetica, Taking Wing	30
Ain't Nobody Going to the Dairy Queen	31
Wolf Hymn	32
A Joyful Noise	33
We Keep Trying to Locate Ourselves in These Woods	34
Super Flower Blood Moon	35
The Trouble with Étienne Brûlé's Hat	36
Lake Superior	37
Mandan Mother Tongue	38
Copper Dog	39
We Tremble Before the Coming Dream	40
Love Is Made from Laughter, Fists, Tears, and Forgetting	41
Fool's Spring	42
Hell and Gone Is a Passing Notion	43
Lane Cove Sirens	44
Rabbit Snares	45
Blood Sonnet	46
Homespun Stitches	47
The Mosquito Inn	48
Mouths to Feed	49
Hushful and Still Closer Comes the Red Fox	50
We'll Learn to Kindle a Slight Blue Flame	51
Elegy	52
In the Bone-Cracking Cold	53
After Dark, We Would Swim Naked	54

Over the Horizon	55
Upon Our Skins. Writhing, We Lost Ourselves	56
A Sixth Great Lake	57
Resilience	58
Manitou	59
Birch Oil, Smoke, Pine Tar, Switch	60
Broken Cartographies	61
Afterword	62
Winter Solstice	63
Acknowledgments	65

A GOOD OMEN

On this first day of the new year, a young crow traps her head
between two narrow pickets in the garden fence, and you
rush outside to free the bird before she snaps her own neck.

You in your black sweater, silver hair lifting behind you
in the cold wind, certainty in your cerulean eyes.

The crow, liberated, exulting from your upraised hands
into a tangled thicket of future hopes and sorrows.

I'M TOLD IT'S FOOLISH TO BEFRIEND A WATER LYNX

Roiling bitter at dusk, the lake spirit rides in
        from the northeast upon a light too faint to speak—
              all breaking whitecap and red, beating heart. Inside
        the cabin, cedar tea simmers in the kettle,
the sauna burns hot, and there is room for one more.
        Cautious, I extend my hands to cup the stories,
              hoping I don't drown in waters I can't fathom.

BEFORE THE FALL

If I could read the ticker tape clacking
from between your clenched teeth, fathom the words
inscribed there, I might snap my fingers bright
in the light moment, crack the lock on this
bone box, and tattoo you again in moons
above the velvet of my trembling fear.
Would you help wipe away the weeping ink
with your heart, rewind the spring assembly
to set broken gears in motion? Luna
moth, candlelight, this night of stars, the hiss
and stink of singed hair. I wear juniper
against moments like this, to remind me
        of when we first rose flushed, grand, and naked
        from the dark waters of this hidden lake.

OURS ARE THESE OLD STAMP MILLS

Nowhere sliced thin to the bone—mnemonic geographies, outer rim reminders, the chemistry of obscure state statistics.

Just out of sight, we're out of our minds, wandering aimlessly down the muddy margins between saltbox houses, between the echo of penny candy, arcade fire.

The school bus driver was a preacher thrown from the pulpit for a secret, while the children leer out the emergency door window making faces and flipping the bird.

Give 'em a wave.

BOTTLED LETTERS TO FORMER LOVERS

Across this turbulent inland sea, we briefly
sailed, howling into the wind. Or was it only
an echo? I dreamt a far shore, flowering trees,

while the captain's quarters burned. Through broken windows,
gaudy children waved chapped little hands, grinning
gap toothed under a brightly glowing sky. Matchstick

and gasoline, that's me, a raging tire fire,
shameless and dirty against the coming cockcrow.
How far into us can I press my dirty thumbs

before hitting bone? It's a parlor trick to ask
a poultice of mud and shit to draw out poison,
but I'd apologize, all the same, for dragging

you beneath these waves with me. I've been a-sinking
and this ship will drown even the strongest swimmers.

WAVE AFTER WAVE

Dawn, a lit fuse. The radioman says
"bombogenesis," like agates tumbling
from a jar—system as meteorite
off Whitefish Point. In other words, water

lynx, *Mishipeshu*, lathered up in red.
In a heartbeat, rollers mass two stories
trough to insatiate tempest, unquelled
by prayer nor cigarette, careless, mean,

a cold-blooded indifference so pure,
a strong swimmer won't last ten wet minutes.
At the Keweenaw, surf pummels the stamp
sands with ocher fists, ore boats stack up lee

of the stone, and entire beaches stand up
to walk away. At Marquette, two lovers
walk onto Black Rocks, sacrificial lambs—
their bodies will never be recovered.

INTO THE THICKET

We go looking for tea cedar, crow feather, and first snow
to stick, but find the mud still warm under our feet, the earth's
moist breath still fogging the looking glass this late into fall.

Deep in our bones, we know we'll waltz on over the frost moon
before the first big freeze cracks ironwood, and the hunkered
sun, low in her cross-quarter nest, fades into dim solstice.

The wind hag is just now beginning her November dance,
pirouetting north, Superior throbbing her meter
deep into the basalt below and beyond simple ken.

Deep in our bones, we feel the forest vibrate in omen,
but as we've no one near to confide in, we must worry
our best wishes, casting spells against the coming darkness.

BEACH GLASS

Shivering in the morning light, we gather like cigarette butts at the water's edge, our thousand naked bodies in a long chain bent from burden and burned to the filter. What we've learned, scars are replaced with more scars, and hair grows up from scorched earth. Once, we would have cut ourselves with broken glass so the wind might rush through the breach to line us with fallen limbs and leaves. But beach sand has since worn dull the sharper edges of our pain. Stomachs empty and growling, we've come at last to these shores copper wired, gear and pulley, all coiled spring and iron will, our words tin typed on our tongues. We clasp arms and dive in together, electric, and beautiful as bullets. We disappear beneath the lake's surface for what seems a grateful eternity, knowing somewhere out beyond the tree line's dark reflection, where the water is cool, clean, and clear, the long arc of a sandbar awaits us.

WRAP THE NEXT HOUR IN RICE PAPER

Too few for bestiary, we sacrifice our birds before they nest.
Little gatherings, little instruction sets, we rummage around.
Sometimes life is pit fruit and we chip a tooth.
Keep the naming eye level with the prize.
Keep everything tight like grandma's rag rugs.

Poised upon a rocky ledge, persisting like cats at a feather under a door,
we guard our cabinets of curiosities like our lives depend on it.

    Our lives depend on it.

LITTLE SPIRITS

We understand them as ambivalent at best, seldom protecting us *from*, more often the cause *of*. Crossed, they are our minor disasters. Untamed, unnamed, we understand them to be whispering in the walls, standing next to the washing machine in our Michigan basements, or sitting on the counters of our ramshackle kitchens, watching us measure out coffee or bleach, dress our children, squeeze out our toothpaste, climb into our sheets. In our gardens, they mark what we will grow and how we will kill. In the forest, they mind their own. They care for us like no one else ever could or they care for us not at all.

BODY AS BURNING BUSH, ALL THE SNAKES

crawling out—blue moon and the sacred grove.
Other times, the eyesore. Spoor along the track.

Lunar, phasing, I'm: (a) pacing, placing
found feathers into an old coffee can; (b) leaning
into the waves, shoulders bent to the paddle.

Heart as the red squirrel, twitching and wary.
Heart as the rain-swollen creek eating the earth.
Heart as the agate, lake polished, found,

        then skipped back into Lake Superior.

NEARING THE END OF THE ANTHROPOCENE

and pursued by apprehension, there is still much to hold on to. Ever the earth hovers about us, whispering its dreams into our tin ears. We have not yet forgotten how to make the crossing, nor how to move with cunning through the shadowed hills, mindful of the signs, attentive to the contours and currents of the land and water from which we were conceived.

LAND ACKNOWLEDGMENT, 1842 CEDED TERRITORY

Rooted in song, these infinite nations
under cathedral woodland dome boundless,
deep as memory, tall as a story
spun moon to sun, salt to sweet water sea,
winter from autumn, summer from springtime,
leaf and needle dancing around the drum,
sugarbush to trout stream to good berry.

Together now, *zagaakwaa ezhaayin*,
    the forest is dense where you are going.

Then snake, the booze hag jig, the winking eye.
Mowed down to cord and plow, built mine and rail,
burned bar and blade—give an inch, give a mile,
give a swollen river of blood. Gutshot
and whitewashed, we still can't find the beat,
and no one can flourish atop this land
acknowledgment. This path is black and charred.

Together now, *zagaakwaa ezhaayin*,
    the forest is dense where you are going.

Patience as weapon, wheel, and medicine—
in the hushed stillness of the seventh dawn
we will paddle toward the east as one,
backs bent forth to an island green and lush.
Between the crow's return and chorus frog,
gather up mother's tongue. *Wiigwaas, giizhik,
maananoons*—no such thing as a trash tree.

Together now, *zagaakwaa ezhaayin*,
    the forest is dense where you are going.

MAKE THE SHAPE OF MICHIGAN WITH YOUR HANDS

Good children don't swim in dead lakes. They don't congregate like shell casings along the line of sand and water. Good children don't stare too long into the darkness or ask questions they shouldn't. They don't play on pavement cracked and weed choked or shade themselves in the shadows of creaking vats or idle along the chain-link long enough to draw attention to themselves. Good children don't drink from cloudy water or wade for minnows and frogs in the shallows—there are no minnows and frogs in the shallows. Neither are there summer dances upon the island like long ago when the young strung lights from the branches of trees and small boats ferried girls in white toward music and laughter across the water. Nothing is across the water. Good children know this and do as they are told.

AT THE MOUTH OF THE GRATIOT

the water is high over the nonesuch shale
and bloodred with hemlock and cedar tannin.

A whisky jack worries my kit for something shiny—
I feast his shadow and he flits away into the forest
on a sudden breeze off Lake Superior.

In just a few days the last leaves will fall,
snow will soon follow, and the land's face will grow quiet.

This river is still well-heeled in rainbows,
the sky isn't yet crashing down.

UP IN UNCANNY VALLEY

my lovers strain and headache, all junkies,
a midnight tightrope act in spurs, uncouth,

feet suspended down into black, pinkies
up. Yours or mine? I want it in the mouth.

Give me the donkey sauce, Guy Fieri,
while fruit flies buzz the wine barrels and fat

girls tear their lips from cigarettes to scare
the last feral act. Won't you come for that?

Yank the bear's head from the water gasping,
young and naked in uncanny valley,

my lovers clutch work quietly asking
what time is it, black dahlia, blind alley?

So be it, this day, our flesh so blue bruised,
in lust, I'm afraid, we're all of us screwed.

OUT BACK OF THE CAMP

It hurts, this walking, weeping wound,
this cleaning up with whiskey, this burning
what's left in a fifty-gallon can. The draw
between is slow and tight. Keep it close,
shut, together. Keep it in the family,
like our mouths and minds. Together,
we'll bleed this bear of its bad blood.

THIS SURVIVAL KNIFE IS ALL WE'LL NEED

to make it in the wilderness. We've been all day at the saplings, carving sticks for tiger pits, squirrel ears nestled like raisins beneath a pommel with a broken compass. Whirling, white-eyed, and shirtless, a violence scratching its balls and sniffing its fingers, we'll take our stitches silently in the kitchen—thank you very much—just a sewing needle, some fishing line, a lighter, and a bottle of whiskey. Put that in your tourist brochure.

OUTSIDE THE U.P. PUB, CALUMET, MICHIGAN

They've got you in their eye beams. Picturing you
in their mind's eye. Spying with their little eye,

pink eye, weak eye, cross eye, stink eye.
I spy the evil eye. Let me look it in the eye.

Let me kiss your eyelid, lick your eyeball.
Let me taste your eye candy, eat your eye bright.
    Feast for the eyes—that's you.

Seeing with both eyes open, left, right,
eyes peeled for the eye of the needle in the haystack,

the straw that'll break the camel's back. On errant eyelashes,
this business of making wishes, of keeping one eye

to the advantage while the other eye stays on the prize.
This business of eye for an eye—I'd give my eyeteeth, bright eyes,
    for another way out.

FOLLOWING THE FOOLS' COUP D'ÉTAT

I ditch the truck in the dirty snowbank
at the fork in Pilgrim and Paradise,
and wander up the ridge into hemlock
whispers, rill song, and a bone ache to heed.

Gunshots echo throughout the forested hills,
peckerwoods, tin toy soldiers pretending
at patriots, not a mask among them—
smallpox blankets still, on brand howbeit.

In the thick gloam of cedar swamp below,
a fellow survivor rattles his horns,
gruffs his scorn at my own entries and breaks,
all the sour notes so soon into the new.

        Grifters and mugs, I shout back, and to hell
        if I can muster anything better.

ETCHED IN GEMSTONE AND ANTLER

The past won't hear our apologies
and the future needs more than a poem.

Amid the gathering silence, safe in our most basic cells,
our hearts release their sacred holdings—
little haloed echoes, etched in gemstone and antler.

Still, we find traces of laughter in the night sky,
feeling like a season following forest fire.

WE SHED OUR CLOTHES LIKE LEAVES

from a tree, less mirror than doorway, a visage less ourselves than gooseflesh migrating across vast expanses of skin. Our flock reveals more than human terms allow. Splashed against the backdrop of stunted shrub and lichen, our chimera's mouth, stifled by feathers, cannot be heard by closing the eyes. Instead, the eyes must squeeze shut, tighter and tighter until the creation of their own white light and the blood roaring into our ears conjures fire, different from conjecturing fire. This is synesthesia, our correction, necessary like pinching ourselves hard between thumb and forefinger over and over, necessary for us to summon up the hot thrum of our bodies, the shushing sound of waves and threshing wind. This place we call elsewhere, anywhere but here, a northern lake, where we swim out beyond the tree line's reflection to a place we know cannot be depended upon. Here we release our buoys from their chains so we might display our illuminated objects.

THE DROWNED FOREST SWALLOWS HIM

In this primitive
spring barely after ice out,
before the peepers,
dogtooth, or birthroot burst forth,
an eight-year-old boy is lost

gathering firewood
along the Big Carp River.
For two days and nights
the drowned forest swallows him
whole. The wind catches its breath.

Sleeping under brush
and eating snow, the boy lives,
and on the third day
the drowned forest returns him
with a wink. The wind exhales.

THEY SAY NOT TO SPEAK OF THE NEGATIVES

like the roof caving in, or the bottom
dropping out. I wonder what to speak of.
Sermons and inside jokes, inscrutable

incantations? The future frightens me.
Flooded *and* parched. I have calculated
the paradox, worried threadbare the slopes

rising ahead, the chart's unknown places.
Somewhere deep in my sheltered bones I see
lost children wandering a burning wood.

JUST ABOUT EVERYTHING BEGINS WITH A LUMP

In the womb, in the armpit, in the throat—nodes on a branch
that become leaves that die and drift to the ground,
leaving bare limbs under a dusting of early snow.

Play something dirge and drudge, trot out the pipes and the strings.
Make a show of forefinger and thumb—*ain't that how it goes,
the world's smallest violin?*

Mostly, it's just a second ago. She's across the table,
sipping a cold beer, smoking a cigarette, pushing greasy hair
behind her greasy ear. Then she isn't.

      Mostly, things are like this. Not holy, just hollow.

FOURTEENER FOR THE RESTLESS IN THE LONG NIGHT

After everything. Broken bottles, bottomed out stumbling
over fumbled buckles, mumbled passions calling collect.
Lying alone, me and my echo shrill in the dark hills—
my voices filtered through broken car speakers, a scratchy

seventy-eight at thirty-three and a third—woman don't
you cry for me—through the wax in my cauliflower ears.
I'm all pillow talk, no fucks left, yet the years keep tripping
by like a primal scream. Why would that be? The Cliff View Bar,

the fallow fields, the dead black farms under stars and more stars,
all the soft bulletins falling to the floor like ashes.
The upholstery is catching fire. It smells bad, my love,
like hair burning, like cabbage wisdom fogging up the glass.

Me in my thin skin, in the elastic black before dawn,
tracing a figure on the glass with my middle finger,
grinning like a pine marten in the flickering torch light.
Here, the rage I hold high above my head, playing for keeps.

Here, the hedge witch begins unwinding the tightly rolled ball.
What a sad song spun from sugar to the clamor of tin,
Me, singing it anyway—can't help myself—unsteady,
held up like a barely managed unkindness of ravens.

THERE ARE PLACES TO HUNT

There are places to hide. Love clicks on and off like a lighter. Love is another word for people. Sometimes the people are trout lilies. Other times, they're a murder of crows. Kissing each other's bodies, we cross our wires to test our hearts. All huddle and quake, we lie with our fingers inside one another, whispering aphorisms into our pillows. When we sleep, it is half sleep. When we dream, we fall down into the belly of an abandoned copper mine. In the morning, we rise from our musk like children. In rolling waves of laughter, we rise to greet whatever sky awaits.

OUT HERE, WE'RE ALL OF US CRACKED

porcelain dolls, cutters and bleeders,
bored as cattle, sitting in the weeds at the edge
of the forest, the sky like a cold trencher.

Smoke and ash, our third eyes watch for black helicopters,
crow orbits, collapsing stars all gamma and radio pulse,
like birdsong, our voices burlesque in their exultation.

Or wild-eyed, shards of broken glass, buried
like barbed wire in the meat of wolf trees, our night terrors
embroidered skyfall, thunderbolt, and mushroom cloud.

A shock wave rippling across the lake, our gravity is a dance
beautiful as bullets, bringing down disaster no less now than ever,
always and never a circle—*what would you know of us?*

That our river has swept beyond its banks.

MISTAKES WERE MADE

I'm too early or two centuries late,
but damn if I don't look good in a hat.

I wanted the hours to keep up the lie,
time licking like pagan alcohol lit

under my rib cage. Dumb shit that I am,
I believed in the bright blue flame of myth.

If I kept thrusting into her belly,
it would feel like true love, faked to be made,

but quick to burn into no never mind.
The past, it comes up quick and electric

in the current. Am I to be beetle
or stone, bright, broken, or whole? All joking

aside, I'm a cup of black coffee set
on the sill. Through the open window, bells.

ARS POETICA, TAKING WING

ain't the hot piece it once was. Tenacity,
just a dog at a bone in blind, mad winter—
there's still some virtue in merely trudging on.

Listen to those birds! Look, the pattern of stars!

Chasing what we can't have, but I say, *cheers!*, lift a glass.
All these ridiculous poems just keep drifting up, and god bless 'em,
the whole rotten racket blowing in on every whiff of breeze.

I do love the screaming.

AIN'T NOBODY GOING TO THE DAIRY QUEEN

In the shadow of the sawmill, of the stamp mill, of these forested hills, we're going to shout, bellow, borrow, and steal—testify! Get a belt, get a switch, knock heads, black an eye, puke blood, froth and seethe, all the gnashing of these false teeth.

On a three-wheeler, buried under Old Style, a man-can in one hand, a child in the other, pinch lipped and liquor puckered, she wants us to know she's not looking for us. We ain't looking for her, neither. Neither running nor feared, and never you mind, son.

She's pounding ham handed against the glass—*for the love of Christ, get that balloon out of your mouth like I told you, or ain't nobody going to the Dairy Queen.*

WOLF HYMN

Wandering in Delirium Wilderness
until blood orange behind the white pine,
cumulus boiling black up off the big lake, north,
nightfall, bush click, a little Old Crow, a lit match.

When the first wolf spirits her prelude skyward,
we jump from our skins, slither up alongside the note
into starburst and a rising, antlered moon,
pay our ancestors amid the thunder and void.

Then polyphonic, the pack of them, their chorus
swelling back into our darkest tunnels
where we have bellied down to listen
in a language almost forgotten, but not lost.

A JOYFUL NOISE

We stumble together up the dirt track
toward the old apple grove, a boom box
and a brown bag between the two of us,
if nothing else. She mumbles, *no good songs*

playing. I point at the darkening trees
and whisper, *let's get lost.* Amid the rocks
at the tumbledown homestead, we fill up
our eager cups to the brim with concert

in minor key, the only that we know,
our feral voices blanketed by starshine.

WE KEEP TRYING TO LOCATE OURSELVES IN THESE WOODS

between the trees / behind wood piles / we descend into cedar swamp / duck into their dark closets / pull our hair shirts up over our heads / hide our faces behind our calloused hands / outside the casino the snow is falling / we smoke discarded cigarette butts and shake / looking over our shoulders for women informants / looking over our shoulders for men from our pasts / looking over our shoulders for ghosts of little darlings / looking over our shoulders for our mothers and fathers and sisters and brothers / looking over our shoulders for our illegitimate children and long-lost dogs / looking over our shoulders for our preachers and parole officers / the shadows threaten to overcome us

SUPER FLOWER BLOOD MOON

Nothing feels particularly super about today,
though as it is like any day in America, blood
is timely beyond shadow of a doubt. Here,
it is always the anniversary of a murder, or
of someone getting away with murder. Mirage
of elliptical orbit and dust, lilies on a grave,
the naked eye prone as it is to pattern making,
and I forget—is it red sky at night, am I to delight
or take fright? Wonder, just another word for terror.

THE TROUBLE WITH ÉTIENNE BRÛLÉ'S HAT

Having professed his deep love for language to Samuel de Champlain, and having spent many years living among the Wyandot-Huron, it seems reasonable to imagine the Frenchman Étienne Brûlé calling his toques by a Wyandot word I cannot locate, lost as I am in these woods.

Standing above what were the great rapids at Sault Ste. Marie, where the immensity of Lake Superior empties into Lake Huron through a series of titan, mechanized locks, I conjure Brûlé's hat as tricornered, insouciant, and rakishly cocked, but I suppose it was a simple affair of fur.

Here we are, though already by the Beaver Wars, our bloodbath had overrun, much has drowned in the centuries between, and while I cannot know in what season Brûlé stood like a first marionette upon these shores, it was probably cold, like today, and he would have been in need of a good hat.

Across the St. Marys, on the Canadian side, they would call his hat a *tuque*, while here in Michigan's Upper Peninsula, I would name it a *tchugue*, but odds are Brûlé must have stood shoulder to shoulder with not just Wyandot but Anishinaabeg upon whose land this is, and thus *wiiwakwaan* might be the best last word.

LAKE SUPERIOR

Under my hand, a stone bear in nesting
circles carved by ancestors, behind me,
the walking woods at dusk, feather and fur,
the little stone, moss, and mushroom people—
we all still and hush to look and listen.
Beyond the barrier islands and reefs,
where the sun sets bloodred and thunderbirds
brew black and quickening, the abyssal
heartbeat spirits deep within the bedrock
upon which all this dreaming is hand sown.
I would call you by your first given name,
Anishinaabewi-gichigami.
> I would make this offering on this ground,
> but what are words against the coming gale?

MANDAN MOTHER TONGUE

no longer clicks and whirs,
nor spins thirst into fairy tale
sparking brush fire.

In the deepening gloom, the clocks
have stopped and the doors
have fallen from their hinges.

Here we bend spoons
with our minds, our dreams
painted in thunder and antimony.

Near the lake a wolf tree,
inexplicable, holds its cards
close to its chest.

COPPER DOG

To run so riotously harnessed to the work of living
as a sled dog at the gangline, twitching out of his own skin
in anticipation of more—more joy, more pain—watertight

to the growling fatigue of the whole damned thing. Call it a pact.
Call us a pack. Fated, dogged, unhinged, this adrenal sprint
through a dark timberland with just a headlamp as harbinger,

ranging along on belief, all of us baying at the moon.
I don't find god in much, but a spoonful sweetens the wheeler
who nips at my bare hand as I haul him into the rigging.

> There's always some blood in the snow—*line out!*—that's just how it
> goes.

WE TREMBLE BEFORE THE COMING DREAM

I shot my best friend in the back of the head, freeing her
from the pain slowly gnawing her guts from the inside out.

Bang and starburst, echoes and soft bulletins shivering
at dawn in the dim light under the forest canopy.

We tremble before the coming dream, before dirt and time,
some new purpose. May we all be so loved as that damned dog.

LOVE IS MADE FROM LAUGHTER, FISTS, TEARS, AND FORGETTING

Blood gone scab is the richest portion of the bone. This land, copper islands, a bottle of vinegar, and behind that nothing, no one, just ghosts. The sun sets over the big lake, a coyote howls in the distance, and the children are lost. Something is forgotten and left behind—distance and time, language, avoidance, and denial. Somewhere a mass grave has been dug. This is head trauma, or gutshot, or running a snowmobile through thin ice, or driving it through some barbed wire, or falling headlong into a swollen river, or tumbling down an abandoned mineshaft, or it's only a tumor and nothing more. How long will each of us lie pondering the sky while our sacred waters run out, while the leaves pile up, while all the love gets made?

FOOL'S SPRING

I've taken to long walks with Walt—the dog ambling ahead,
long and lean—one torn page of mud song at a turn.

Aflame along the Salmon Trout and swift down to Freda
the forest creeps rebellious through crack and crevice
where a wreck of smokestack mumbles through a mouthful of stars.

High above in the nave, the blue jay is Psalm—
Steal the day, he sings, *and hold on tightly to each other.*

HELL AND GONE IS A PASSING NOTION

My glass never was more than half empty,
the grass yonder a shade greener. Sordid

details, let's call it brush fire burning
out of control, desire like a klaxon
screaming run, a rot lodged deep down under
the skin. But blood, gear, or pulley won't budge
the moon in her orbit, and rolled up tight,
black magic doesn't just smolder, it blasts
the dweller in white-hot cinder and ash,
leaving in its wake a deep smoking pit

that won't fill back in so easy. They say
how hell and gone is a passing notion,
that some leave to behold stars once again,
but that's a dose tough to cook in a spoon.

LANE COVE SIRENS

We paddled out from Belle Isle at dawn, bellies bulging with lake trout, beards glistening with the grease, pleased as punch behind our teeth, beneath our strong backs, able before the gathering gods, and slid before the gale into the sudden calm of the cove.

Then a sound, a ricochet off the water, some flute note from the forest, or a stray breeze playing along a fishing line, somewhere between gunwale and the rippling water.

       Again, soft, submelodic, something just out of reach. *Can you hear it?*

For an hour we floated in the falling light, branches bent to drift and loon call, into and out of the mystery, silently searching the crystal depths between logjam and moose bone to savvy, but finding only our own gooseflesh, and grateful for it.

RABBIT SNARES

Small
hands
taught well
to set snares
carefully along
the path—rabbit as a person
of ceremony, just like you and me. Movable,
this feast under the blazing Milky Way. When he trips the noose,
      his reciprocity
opens a small hole in space-time through which a murmuration of ancestors
      pour—their words, gratitude in whatever language they whisper.

BLOOD SONNET

Near the Yellow Dog, a small child stands framed
in the crooked doorway of a cabin.
Something in the matted blond hair, dirty
bare feet, homespun shift, the tremulous hand
shading hollow eyes from a badger sun.
Motionless for the Brownie, some dark thing
hides behind the heavenly, sour and ill
at ease—that young'un cut his own switches.
What the blackflies can't take out in cold blood,
a black bear can finish with thievery.
Come winter, he'd learned to boil his boots.
Come spring, his mother'd be dead from trying.
> *So many spirits named in candle flame*
> *inside the closed circle of memory.*

HOMESPUN STITCHES

the Thorazine drag
all buckets of rusty nails
rickets and wolf spider

love is rabid bit
love is strapped to a gurney
laugh it off, my love

THE MOSQUITO INN

We walked in laughing at our hairy potbellies, sharing another cigarette. If we could have put away our pocketknives long enough, we would have ended up in bed, shouldering each other's weight around the soiled sheets.

Let's false promise to walk that line, pinky swear. Let's pretend we have no intention to hang ourselves. That's some kind of song, ain't it, come to rest on hands and knees, head hung low, and panting?

Lucky in our love, like old radios on windowsills, our dusty vacuum tubes still warm to the pinch of electricity.

Our volume still turns up too loud.

MOUTHS TO FEED

Mouths to wash out with soap, to fill with words
to be thrown back at us like bricks.

The garden has gone to weeds.
The garage needs painting.
The brakes on this old pickup will give at any second.

It's all been so long coming, is so much anticipated,
it will end in an enormous exhalation of relief.

We must learn to be hungry, to keep company with it,
to know what it means to drive directionless in pursuit

       of something gnawing,
       of something empty.

HUSHFUL AND STILL CLOSER COMES THE RED FOX

and chickadee, the turning of thistle
and thorn—I reach up into memory
tidally locked and phasing like moonglow
overhead, or deep down into greenstone
billions of years beneath the trillium.

I've scant to say that's not already sung
by the wind in the balsam and cedar,
or the stones at the bend of the river.

       The steady beat of our own wolfish hearts.
           The chorus that is starshine in our eyes.
               The land that speaks when we've ears to listen.

WE'LL LEARN TO KINDLE A SLIGHT BLUE FLAME

In this middle passage, the morning sun
        is strong upon the water.
                No one else for miles

to bless this thing, only the sound of waves
        and threshing wind, our voices
                raised alone in song

for each other. Our good hearts to shake off
        the falling darkness, bearing
                into a world bent

against us. No one wins–laugh them off, love.
        Huddled close within, bound tight,
                together we'll learn

to kindle a slight blue flame, cradle it
        like a songbird's egg, all soft
                procedure and steel

will, listening as one for the crystal
        call to shed at last our husks
                and laud into light.

ELEGY

Up from brown water at the bottom of a honey bear,
we drove your rusty rez Chevy out to the Capitol
to free Peltier, higher than cirrus, all pepper and piss.

First night, a Dakota elder read aloud my skinny,
white ass—you laughed so hard you tipped into the dirt, slept wrapped
in your long black hair. None of it tracked, man. My beard, so gray

all of a sudden. Peltier, still rotting in his prison.
Then one cold winter day on a Colorado glacier,
you took your life. I look up into these rising blue hills,

up into the hoard of stars, none of it makes any sense,
not in a language I will ever understand. Most days
since walking off into the dust, your grinning shadow drapes

a thick arm round my shoulders. Side-eyed I can catch a glimpse,
your spirit like a lake breeze blowing through crowns of white pine,
whispering, *hey, fool, whatcha gonna do with yourself now?*

IN THE BONE-CRACKING COLD

On this cross-quarter day, quick to temper and cool,
your long lashes startle me with a rime of hoarfrost,

and I am snared like a rabbit pulled into your gravity
by nature of our long love affair. The seasons race by,

one after another, rising sap soon to halo the maples again,
but I would freeze in the bone-cracking cold, just to watch

you walk slowly through the sugar bush, rare as a sun dog
incandescent in the softly falling snow, forever.

AFTER DARK, WE WOULD SWIM NAKED

We were going to quit smoking, quit coffee, quit drinking—remember? But what would have remained to keep us from killing? Hell, I would have quit books, too, but I would have had to start my sunburned life over again. Under our pillows we had been stashing all the ache in our teeth, the longing for each other's skin, the ten thousand noticings of shore and forest, that which contained us as we contained one another. After dark, steaming from the sauna, we would swim naked out into the black water, withdrawing and pushing away from ourselves, floating on our backs, hands crossed over our hearts, staring up into a fathomless Milky Way. And afterward, wrapped in wool blankets, we would sit on the porch, watching as new snow descended slowly down onto our haloed heads, each of us silent in prayer.

OVER THE HORIZON

is more horizon. Down the logging road is more logging road.
Some dreams deserve to be run down, while others deserve to escape.
Up here, we know how to tell the time.

UPON OUR SKINS. WRITHING, WE LOST OURSELVES

Not what we once were, wrapped tight in stinging
nettles, lottery cards etched in bad blood
upon our skins. Writhing, we lost ourselves
and balanced on wires like birds—as we were.

Catastrophes awaited us. If hard-pressed,
I'd speak a name or three, but climb too far
into the twilight of my obsessions
and you'll find me fixed alone and lonesome.

After all was said and done, we walked
to the point to look deep into the dark
depths of the bay. The sun had disappeared
from view, but it wasn't too late to see
across to home, not yet. And though we spoke
in crippled tongue, we still knew a few words.

A SIXTH GREAT LAKE

Often hidden from view,
our teachers come in strange garb—
one dressed in trillium,
another as black bear.

Be humble and hungry, she says,
hold out your hands. Make more,
be grateful, live and give freely.

Slow now. Listen to the light.
Keep the water.

RESILIENCE

How to hang a door, hold a chain saw, or hammer a nail. How to butcher a hog, bed a lover, and bury a baby. How to change a tire, a lightbulb, or a diaper. How to build a fence, a fire, or a family. How to dig a grave and dry tears. How to tie a knot, a tie, a fly, and/or one's own noose. How to point a well, plant a garden, and pluck a chicken. How to boil water, birth a calf, and mend a broken heart. How to shovel a path, split a log, and square a post. How to aim a shotgun, salt the earth, stanch the flow of blood. How to gather cedar, chaga, make a cup of tea. How to weather a storm and write a song. How to say you're sorry. How to heal. How to live in that good way. How to die in that good way.

MANITOU

Where we yearn most, thunderbirds
nest, our souls thrilling
to their quickening tempest.

Rooted in earth and water,
we raise up our hands
into laceworks of lightning.

BIRCH OIL, SMOKE, PINE TAR, SWITCH

Sweat beads above her trapezius scar,
coalescing to rivulet down her
torso, past the mole I've claimed my own, stone
amid the gathering rush. She reaches
for the pine bucket of water, mother
Superior in her dipping spoon, then
quick wrist flick at the rocks atop the stove,
white hiss of steam mushrooming, rising up
to the low ceiling before circling round,
settling like nettles along the low bench.
Cedar walled, lost in cloud bank, each of us
a gathering, wordless storm, we dewdrop
      and breach in long arcing inhalations
          of lung and heart, time and memory. Slow

now, patience, stamina, suffering, charge.
Another time, shore, and sauna, she slipped
on wet tile and fell atop a wood stove,
searing metal branding deep into her
a burn so bad she did not even hurt,
leaving her the scar, shaped like Michigan's
Upper Peninsula. A sign. This day,
this afternoon, our ten thousand secrets
between us, reflections mirrored perfect
in the ice-cold blue of the lake outside.
As close as I'll come to church—birch oil, smoke,
pine tar, switch, ritual cycle of fire,
      sweet water. As close as I'll come to god—
      her body, gold, red maple leaves falling.

BROKEN CARTOGRAPHIES

We mark our maps in musk, dust, woodsmoke, and urine, disoriented to the polar star.

We stumble into our open topographies in a rage that won't kindle, won't burn, our oxidation too slow for the tasks at hand.

We move through these landscapes as if we weren't born to them, as if these hills and valleys weren't our very own, as if we were lost and might never be found.

AFTERWORD

We sat huddled together cross-legged,
hunched inside a walled city built of books.
All our sordid stories spun in fragment
in tongues bound and gagged to bare belief.
Knowable, but let's face facts, meaningless.

The shiny bits we read over again
like bolts from birds, small fibs brought home to nest,
pretty, useless. Love me with your boots on,
I whisper, a pinky swear hidden deep
in my pocket, two ciggies for after.

Is that too true? Even in the sunshine
under the trees, two cups of steaming tea
in our hands, all the angles remembered—
macerated flowers. Can you smell them?

WINTER SOLSTICE

As the fires of the world
burn to ash and shadow, all
the light seems to fade away.

Even the north wind grows still.
Snow piles up. Crow is silent.
In the deep lake, the lynx sleeps.

Here, we are the aurora.
Come in to help keep the flame
and sing our return to dawn.

Acknowledgments

Thank you to Marika, Ani, Indrek, and all my kith and kin for their love and support.

Thank you to my friends at KBIC, LVD, and Redcliff for their encouragement and gracious gut checks on Anishinaabemowin usage and the limitations of my positionality. Special thanks to Kristin for helping me to understand.

Gratitude to all the teachers.

Thank you to Michigan Technological University for keeping a poet housed and fed, and to all the good people at Wayne State University Press for doing the lord's work.

Certain of these poems—in whole or in part, in different form or under different title—have previously appeared in: *About Place Journal*; *And Here: 100 Years of Upper Peninsula Writing, 1917–2017*; *Barely South Review*; *Barrelhouse*; *Bateau*; *Bluestem*; *Cellpoems*; *DIAGRAM*; *Forklift, Ohio*; *The Fourth River*; *H_NGM_N*; *Isle Royale National Park*; *Lit Up Magazine*; *Lumberyard Magazine*; *Michigan Quarterly Review*; *Monkeybicycle*; *Pamplemousse*; *Poetry*; *Rewilding: Poems for the Environment*; *Split Rock Review*; *TRUSH*; and *Wheelhouse*.

This book is dedicated to Wood.

About the Author

M. BARTLEY SEIGEL is a former poet laureate of Michigan's Upper Peninsula and an Academy of American Poets Laureate Fellow. His poetry frequently appears in literary journals such as *Poetry*, *Michigan Quarterly Review*, *About Place*, *The Fourth River*, and *THRUSH*. He lives with his family on the Keweenaw Peninsula, Ojibwe homelands and Treaty of 1842 territory, where he teaches at Michigan Technological University.

Photo Credit: Adam Johnson